A special thanks to our featured Tiny Thinkers:
Koharu Rosalia Hamlitsch
Melody Bateman
Ella Ripple

Richie Doodles
A Tiny Thinkers Book

Written by: M.J. Mouton
Illustrated by: Jezreel S. Cuevas
Edited by: David Smalley

Production Manager: David Smalley
Art Consultant: Deanie Mouton
Book Design: Nicole Crenshaw

Printed in China

US Library of Congress
ISBN: 9780998314716

Hi, I'm Hitch!

I've spent time with some amazing
Tiny Thinkers! Join me as we learn about
people and the science they discovered.
And see if you can spot me along the way,
as I tell you the story of Richie's real-life
adventure that changed the world!

RICHIE
DOODLES

Written by M.J. Mouton **Illustrated by Jezreel S. Cuevas**

A Foreword by
Lawrence M. Krauss

I am a scientist today because Richie inspired me. He inspired me with his lectures, which made my mind soar. He inspired me with his excitement and enthusiasm about the world.

He inspired me because he had so much fun. He inspired me because he was brave enough to explore the world in ways no one had ever done before.

He inspired me because he wasn't afraid to ask questions, and he wasn't afraid to not know the answer. He inspired me because when he didn't know the answer to something he worked hard to find out.

He inspired me because he knew how to teach himself new things. And, because I was lucky enough to meet my hero while I was still in school, he inspired me because he told me to always seek adventure in life. He also told me to be brave enough to do what I thought was right, and not care what other people think.

Part of the reason I write, and teach and work the way I do is because Richie gave me a wonderful example of how it could be done.

Lawrence M. Krauss,
Theoretical physicist, and writer.

Richie loved math, science, and art.

He questioned something about everything, because he was smart.

He would look at a puzzle from the top to the bottom.

He was okay with not knowing the answer, the fun was solving the problem!

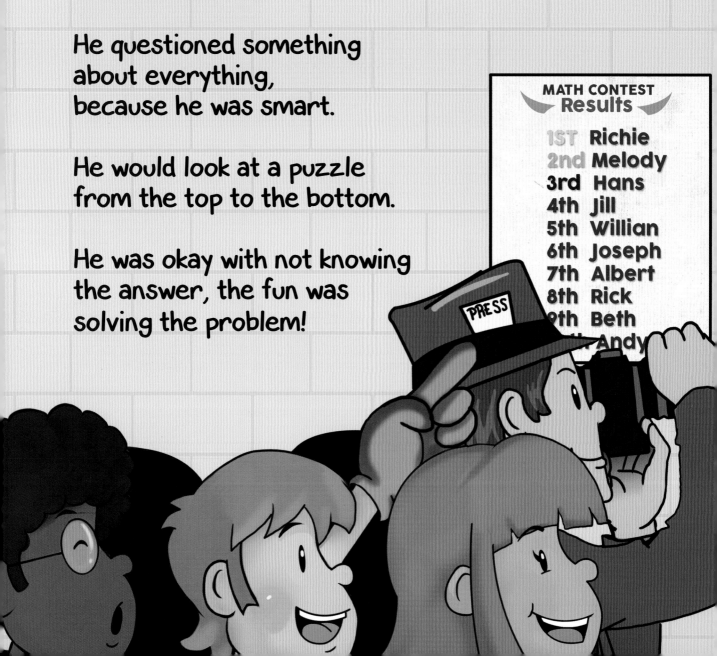

MATH CONTEST
Results

1ST Richie
2nd Melody
3rd Hans
4th Jill
5th Willian
6th Joseph
7th Albert
8th Rick
9th Beth
Andy

Richie's biggest puzzle was about atoms
and the smaller particles inside them.

He knew what they could do,
and how we could find them.

These particles could go upwards, downwards,
and sideways, forwards and backwards,
or this way, and that way.

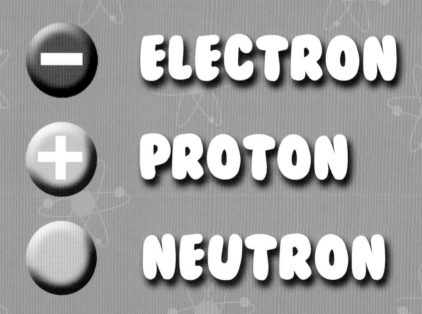

ELECTRON

PROTON

NEUTRON

Richie loved to teach others about
the problems he solved.
He especially liked talking about
things that are small.

If he did not have an answer to a
query, he would say "I don't know"
unless he had a theory.

Sometimes finding the answer is what Richie thought was pleasing.

I bet he could solve problems while he was dreaming!

MUON NEUTRINO
ELECTRON NEUTRINO
ELECTRON NEUTRINO
TAU NEUTRINO
TAU NEUTRINO
MUON NEUTRINO

He had crazy ideas about the smallest things you can fathom. Things smaller than pin points, and smaller than atoms!

Things so small you can't see them at all. Things so small they pass right through walls!

How small are these particles? If you can imagine...
The particles Richie drew could fit inside atoms!

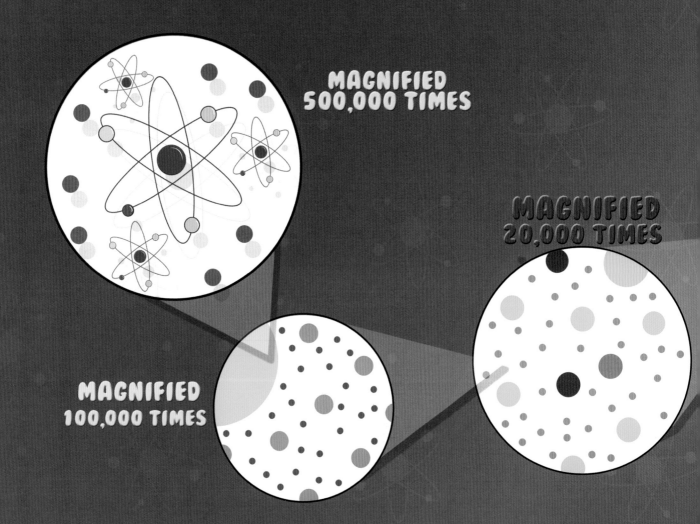

MAGNIFIED
500,000 TIMES

MAGNIFIED
20,000 TIMES

MAGNIFIED
100,000 TIMES

How small is an atom? How many can there be?
There are millions inside specks too small to see.

Hold up your thumb for a second or two, and you can find out what a small particle can do.

Tiny particles pass through
your thumb without slowing.
They do it all the time without
you even knowing!

It takes a whole lot of math
to explain how particles act.

They go this way, and that way,
and that is a fact!

Richie understood these itsy bitsy particles.

He doodled pictures to explain them for science journals and articles.

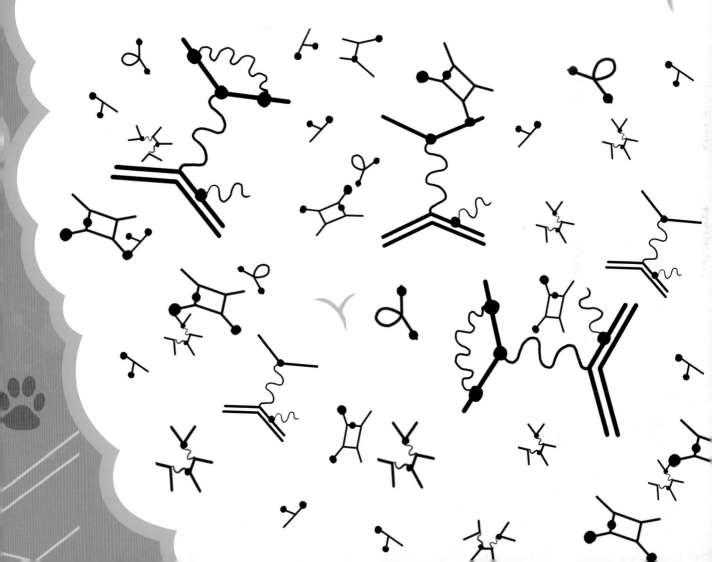

Richie was certainly known for these doodles.
Some had straight lines, and zig-zags,
and squiggles like noodles.

Going upwards and downwards, there were oodles of doodles.

If you stacked them together they might look like a poodle!

Why are these doodles so important you ask?
They explain what happens to the energy when

They show us what particles do when they repel or
attract, in the past, in the future, or forward, and back.

He drew lines that went downward
and upward and sideways.
Lines that went this way,
and that way, and all ways.

Lines that would curve and some lines that had waves...
Joining and splitting is how these particles behave.

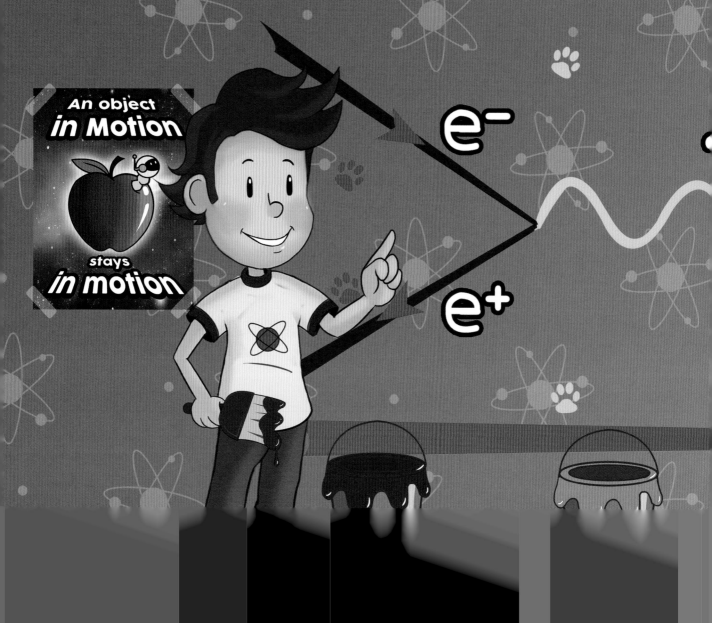

Here is how his doodle works.
One of Richie's doodles can show
what happens when particles touch.

An object
in Motion

stays
in motion

e^-

e^+

An electron and a positron
will destroy each other, not leaving too much.
Only a little bitty light wave that floats without care,
until it turns into a quark and an antiquark pair.

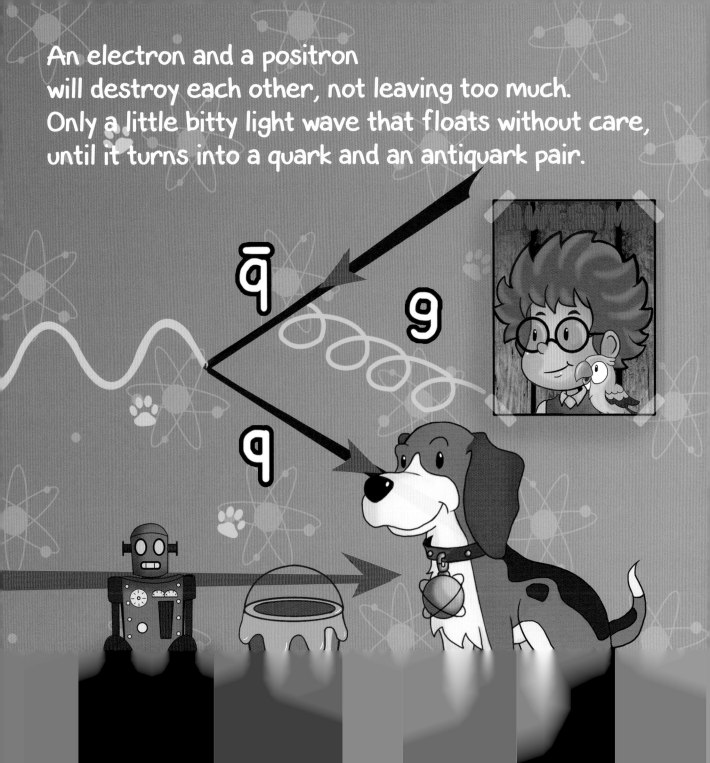

Richie drew oodles and oodles of doodles, explaining particles in a way that is simple and useful.

You may understand particles if you give his doodles a look, instead of jumbled up math problems on chalkboards or in books.

If your teacher sees you doodling in class, and says those silly drawings won't help you pass...

You can explain that your doodle isn't silly at all. It's called a Feynman Diagram explaining things that are small.

You better be able to explain it yourself.
You can find Richie's doodles on library shelves.

If the book is up high, and you can't get it yourself,
ask the librarian, and she will give you some help.

Then you can explain particles that go this way, and that way.
Upwards, and downwards, sideways, and all ways.

With lines that are straight, and curly like noodles.
The smallest of things explained in a doodle.

Richie became famous for his oodles of doodles, and even taught these doodles to oodles of pupils!

The greatest adventure is solving riddles big or small. Richie solved riddles about the smallest of all.

He saw the world from another point of view. Like Richie, the next great riddle can be solved by you!

THE END

Richie grew up to be known as...

RICHARD FEYNMAN

1918-1988